CDM 2015 Explair

CW01498465

By Gavin Taylor

Preface

The Construction (Design and Management) Regulations are one of the least-well understood and complied with pieces of health and safety legislation in Great Britain. That is not to say that everyone gets it wrong, just that so many companies, large and small, ignore the regulations, misunderstand them, sometimes deliberately, or believe that they just don't apply to them. One possible reason for this is the apparent complexity of the regulations and the broad nature of the requirements they contain.

The CDM Regulations changed in April 2015 and this book reflects those changes. This book aims to help you cut through the complexity of the regulations so that you can comply now.

My task in writing this book has been to collate information from several sources, including the regulations, the guidance and published articles and to condense them into one, easy to use resource. You can explore these documents yourself and I would encourage you to read sections of the regulations and the guidance produced by the Health and Safety Executive to confirm that what you understand from this book is true. What you should find is that, after reading this book, finding what you are looking for and putting it into context is so much easier.

While every effort has been made to address the whole construction industry with this book, there are bound to be instances where you have unanswered questions regarding your situation. I encounter such questions when I deliver CDM training courses to companies all over Great Britain and they can only really be answered on a case by case basis. If you have one of those questions, please send it to the author at gavin.taylor@knutsfordsafety.co.uk or contact him through Knutsford Safety LLP.

Table of Contents

Chapter 1 – Introduction

Let's start by quashing a few common misunderstandings. The first incorrect statement is 'CDM only applies to big projects'. No, CDM applies to all construction work, even if it involves just one person doing a few minutes of construction work. The way CDM applies in practice will need to be in proportion to the scope and complexity of the project but it applies to ALL construction work.

The second incorrect statement is 'CDM does not apply to house extensions'. No, CDM does apply to house extensions. The 2015 version of the regulations even applies to 'domestic clients', that's you or I when we ask for a new bathroom to be built in our own home. Other duties apply to the architect/designer and to the builder, electrician, plumber, joiner and all other trades involved in building the house extension.

So, now that we have set a few things straight, let's be clear on why the CDM Regulations exist. The first and simplest reason is because we, in Great Britain, must have these regulations in place. The UK is a member state of the European Union which means that we must implement all relevant European Directives. CDM comes from a European Directive titled the Temporary or Mobile Construction Sites Directive of 1992. The Health and Safety Executive (HSE) wrote the first version of the regulations in 1994 and then revised them in 2007 and again in April 2015.

The second reason for CDM is because it is needed. The construction industry has a poor track record when it comes to health and safety, although the situation has improved in many respects over recent years. We are responsible for a disproportionate number of deaths, injuries and ill-health cases compared to many other industries. Contractors have, for a long time, had direct duties for construction safety set out in legislation. What CDM recognised and changed was the need for other people involved in the construction process to get involved in preventing accidents and ill-health too. Hence, the 'design and management' bit of CDM. Designers are challenged to do more to eliminate and reduce risks through design and clients, as well as others, are encouraged to improve the way that projects are managed to avoid the loss of vital information and to improve planning and teamwork.

This book draws on the Construction (Design and Management) Regulations 2015 available via the government's legislation website www.legislation.gov.uk. Note that health and safety legislation in GB is used for criminal law purposes in that a failure to comply could result in a form of prosecution. The regulation is supported by guidance which is available to download free of charge from the HSE website www.hse.gov.uk. Search for L153 – Guidance on the Construction (Design and Management) Regulations 2015 www.hse.gov.uk/pubns/priced/l153.pdf. The guidance isn't law, but it provides clear direction on ways to achieve compliance. It also provides essential information that helps to make these regulations understandable. If you follow the guidance, much of which is explored in this book, you will normally be doing enough to comply with the law.

Chapter 2 – Definitions

Construction Work

Probably the most important definition to start with is 'construction work'. There really is no substitute for reading this definition in the regulations because it is so extensive. The main point to take from reading the definition is that it applies to far more activities than most people think. As you would expect, all the traditional activities such as excavation, erecting steelwork, cladding, etc. involved in forming the structure are classed as construction work and this is clear. What is surprising is that the upkeep, maintenance, repair, renovation, decoration and some cleaning of the structure may also be classed as construction. The Health and Safety Executive clarified that some activities, such as redecoration and cleaning using a jet wash or abrasive under pressure are only classed as construction when they are undertaken as part of a wider construction project. So, jet washing or grit blasting paving on its own is not construction work, but jet washing or grit blasting a concrete tank before repairing cracks in the concrete would be. Similarly, painting or wall papering a wall would not be construction work on their own, but they would be if the wall was formed in stud partition shortly before being decorated.

The definition of construction work goes on to clarify that putting together or taking apart prefabricated elements to form a structure is also classed as construction work. This could apply to gantries and walkways that bolt together, or to kit-form log cabins. Preparation for construction work is construction too. This includes boreholes, trial pits, clearing buildings ready for construction or felling trees to make way for a structure. However, planting trees and general horticultural work are excluded from this definition. Getting rid of surplus debris and construction material from the site is also classed as construction work. The real surprise is the inclusion of all work to building services whether installing, removing or maintaining them. This means that installing telecoms lines, IT cables, process pipework, even installing a satellite dish are all construction work.

The definition of construction work refers to things being done to structures. 'Structures' is defined in the regulations and includes an impressive list of things including pipes, cables, earthworks and fixed plant. So, any work equipment that has to be fixed in position, such as robots, major metalworking equipment, industrial ovens, large printing press etc., is considered a structure and any work to install, remove, repair or maintain it could be classed as construction work. In the Approved Code of Practice to the 2007 version of the regulations the definition of construction was modified to exclude the general maintenance of fixed plant. This would apply to maintenance activities where guards or elements are designed to be removed easily to facilitate cleaning or replacement. This exclusion would not extend to significant dismantling of large fixed plant such as removing the crown from a large industrial press. Note that this exclusion only applied to fixed plant – not to the other items classed as structures. There is no reason to suggest that this exclusion has changed. The water industry explored this boundary between maintenance and construction and developed guidance on how to differentiate between the two for typical maintenance activities. Their guidance, available via https://www.water.org.uk/guidance/construction-design-and-management/ provides useful direction that can be applied to many other industries.

The erection of temporary structures is also classed as construction. This includes scaffold platforms, formwork and falsework. Previously, the entertainment industry was excluded from the CDM Regulations. However, that exclusion was removed with the introduction of the 2015 regulations. This means that the erection of stages for pop concerts and temporary structures for festivals are classed as 'construction work' and that CDM 2015 will be enforced for those activities.

The regulations also exclude specific industries including mineral or resource extraction, shipbuilding, work on ships and off-shore work as they have their own regulations. A minor change in the regulations clarifies that archaeological survey, i.e. Time Team, carried out before construction work starts is not classed as construction work either. Note also that a homeowner carrying out DIY is excluded from the CDM Regulations.

Client

Another important definition is 'Client'. Anyone who wants construction work to be carried out and either uses their own employees or external consultants and contractors to work on the project is classed as a client. The client is usually the person or company at the top of the procurement chain and will ultimately foot the bill for the work. Just because a contractor engages a subcontractor, this does not make them a client too. Equally, a factory owner who engages a project manager to run a project does not abdicate himself from client duties; he has merely engaged someone to help him fulfil those duties.

Another important definition is 'domestic client'. If you want to extend your home to build a bigger kitchen, purely for your own or your family's use, you are a 'domestic client'. This is because the work to be done has nothing to do with a business or trade. The 'domestic client' may still have duties but you will see later in this book how those duties will normally pass to someone else.

There are a few potential complications to this. What if you work from home or if your home is attached to your workplace? If you extend your home to form an office for work purposes, you no longer qualify as a 'domestic client' and CDM will apply to you as a client. If you are a childminder and convert part of your home into a play area, CDM will apply to you as a client too. Equally, the shop owner who lives above his shop will have client duties for any work to the shop but not to the flat that he lives in unless the flat is also used for work, such as a store. A similar situation exists on farms where any construction work to farm buildings would make the farmer a client. However, work on the purely residential part of the farm with no business-related work would make the farmer a 'domestic client'.

A further complication occurs when the occupier of a residential property is a tenant. The landlord would normally be the client for any construction work done, initiated or arranged by him to the property. However, if the tenant arranges and pays for construction work to improve the rental property purely for their own means, they are a 'domestic client'. If an insurance company arranges for work to be done, they are usually a client with duties under CDM. Many churches or church circuits are in a similar position because they tend to own a domestic property to house the minister/priest. The church is the client for any construction work carried out on the property.

Where a group of residents forms an association to manage the common parts of flats, the association is the client for any work outside the domestic flats or for any common building services. Other unsuspecting clients include school governors, charities, scout groups and sports clubs, to name a few.

A common misunderstanding with the client duties stems from property development, mostly because it is inconvenient to interpret the regulations correctly. All property developers are clients under CDM. If you watch property development shows on television, you will notice that all the contestants aim to make money, this sounds like work, by buying property, refurbishing it and selling it on. This is a business and these individuals are clients. They cannot claim to be 'domestic clients' just because they spend a small amount of time in the property while they are refurbishing it. One test to use here is whether the income from property development is a significant source of income or whether it is incidental to the primary income stream. In short – is this work?

Designer
A designer is defined as anyone who prepares or modifies a design or arranges for or instructs someone under their control to prepare a design as part of their work. Note that you don't need to have the word 'designer' in your job title to be a designer. You could be the client for a project but if you make key design decisions or specify materials to be used, you are also a designer. Similarly, contractors who make material choices, choices over cable routes or design temporary works are designers too. Local Authority planning officers who express a preference (outside of statutory requirements) are designers as well.

The key point to extract from the definition of designer (and subsequent duties) is that anyone who makes decisions or choices that affect health and safety in construction is probably a designer and should make those decisions in a responsible manner. This 'responsible manner' is spelt out in the designer duties.

Notifiable Project

If a project is 'notifiable', this means that the project details must be notified to the enforcing authority, usually the HSE. A notifiable project is one where the construction work on the construction site is scheduled to last longer than 30 working days and have more than 20 workers working simultaneously at any point in the project or exceed 500 person days. This definition changed in the 2015 version of the regulations, as did the impact of a project being notifiable. The biggest change is that when a project is notified, this has no other impact on the project. In the 2007 version of the regulations, if a project was notifiable, this triggered additional duties and additional documents. This is no longer the case. The client simply sends notification of the project to the enforcing authority, possibly with later updates, and then focuses on the rest of the CDM Regulations.

Another change to the definition of 'notifiable project' introduced in the 2015 version of the regulations is a change from the phrase 'likely to' to 'scheduled to'. In the 2007 version of the regulations the notifiability of a project might be re-evaluated during the construction stage if the project was likely to run over the notifiability thresholds by a significant amount. Now, with the introduction of the phrase 'scheduled to', it appears that the notifiability triggers need only be considered before construction starts based on what was scheduled. If the construction phase extends, it could be argued that this does not change what was scheduled to happen at the beginning of the project. Whether this was what was intended by the HSE remains to be seen.

The 2007 version of the regulations used to consider if a project was likely to exceed 30 days of construction work. This has changed because the new threshold considers whether construction work will last longer than 30 days and have more than 20 workers working on site simultaneously at any point in the project. What this means is that fewer projects are notifiable because they will not have more than 20 workers on site at any one time. A day of construction work is defined as any day on which construction work is carried out. Even if only a few hours of construction work take place on a day, this is counted as one day. If a project has a break between two or more phases, the periods when no construction work is carried out do not count towards the total number of days.

The '500 person days' exists to capture short-duration but labour-intensive construction projects. A person day is typically defined as a standard 8-hour working day. In the winter, a worker would typically work just one person day per calendar day. In the summer, a worker could easily work 1.5 person days in one calendar day. If shift working was used, up to three person days could be worked in a day just by having one person on day shift and one on night shift. By the same measure, working until lunchtime on Saturday would only count as half of one person day. Imagine a shutdown at a manufacturing factory. Shutdown periods rarely last longer than two weeks. The construction work must be finished in those two weeks so the '30 days and more than 20 workers' threshold will not be exceeded. However, if there are 12 people on day shift and 12 people on night shift for 14 days to complete the construction work, this exceeds 500 person days (14 days x 2 shifts x (12 persons x 1.5 days) = 504 person days).

Note that projects for domestic clients are now notifiable if they exceed these thresholds. This is different to the 2007 version of the regulations. So now, regardless of the project or the client, all projects that will exceed the notifiability thresholds must be notified to the enforcing authority. This is a client duty.

Project
You might think that there is no need to define the word 'project'. We all know what a project is, but it appears that some people try to avoid some of the thresholds in the CDM Regulations by confusing project and contract. When determining if these thresholds have been exceeded, we have to anticipate the duration of construction work and the number of contractors to complete the project. You cannot count the work to complete the foundations as one project, the structural steel as another and the cladding as another. If any one of them was omitted, this project would be incomplete. So, all the construction work required to get from the current situation to the finished, fully operational structure is one project.

This becomes more complicated for a programme of works such as a collection of similar works at numerous sites for the same client. Very often the client will use similar solutions at each site and let a contract to cover all the work. Such an occurrence is common for utility companies. There is disagreement whether a programme of work is one project. Some advisors will tell you that a programme of works at numerous, physically separated sites is one project. The theory is that they are planned by one team, constructed by one team and are usually funded from the same pot of money. This is hard to argue with, especially when guidance produced by Construction Skills says that projects should not artificially be divided to avoid notifiability. While I disagree with the concept of minor works at lots of sites being classed as one project when considering CDM thresholds, the HSE's own website provides advice on notification for multiple-site projects. So, until something changes, you will have to treat multi-site projects as one project for the purpose of notifiability.

Chapter 3 – Structure of the CDM Regulations

The regulations are divided into five parts. They are:
Part 1 – No title
Part 2 – Client Duties
Part 3 – Health and safety duties and roles
Part 4 – General requirements on all construction sites
Part 5 – No title

Part 1 introduces the regulations, defines several terms and explains when and to whom the regulations apply. There are no duties in part 1 to comply with. In fact, all that part 1 does is to help you decide if CDM applies to your situation. This can be summarised by one sentence in the guidance which states: 'CDM 2015 applies to all construction projects in Great Britain.'

Part 2 focuses on the client duties. Most client duties are collected into one to make them more accessible and easier to understand. This should help those clients who rarely have construction work done to find, read and be able to comply with their legal duties.

Part 3 starts by setting out the general duties common to all duty-holders. Note that some of these general duties will apply to the client as well. Then it describes the duties for each duty-holder and their responsibilities towards the documents required by the regulations. Consequently, this section is most useful to designers, the principal designer, contractors and the principal contractor.

Part 4 contains duties that relate to the physical rather than managerial issues that affect construction sites such as excavations, fire safety and lighting. The duties in part 4 apply to all construction projects, even work on domestic projects.

Part 5 deals with administrative issues such as the transition from the old regulations to the new and authority to enforce the regulations. There are no duties within part 5.

So, all parts of the CDM Regulations apply to all construction projects regardless of size and nature. Regulation 6, the duty for a client to notify, will only apply if a project is notifiable. The duties that relate to a principal designer and principal contractor will only apply if a project is likely to have more than one contractor.

There are five defined duty-holders in CDM and they are:
The client (usually only one but it is possible to have more).
The principal designer (appointed by the client, usually only one but can change during the project).
Designers (anyone who makes design decisions is a designer, no need for appointment).
The principal contractor (appointed by the client, usually only one per site, can change).
Contractors (anyone who carries out or manages construction work as part of their business).

Chapter 4 – Projects with Two or More Contractors

The biggest change introduced by CDM 2015 is the new threshold of whether a project will have two or more contractors during the life of the project. Put simply, every project with two or more contractors will have a principal designer and a principal contractor. This will be the case regardless of the size of the project or whether the project is for a commercial or a domestic client. The client must appoint a principal designer and principal contractor in writing and must do so as soon as is practicable. This means that as soon as any designer is engaged on a project where two or more contractors are likely, a principal designer must be appointed. Equally, as soon as a contractor is engaged to carry out construction work, a principal contractor must be appointed before construction commences on site. If a client fails to appoint a principal designer or principal contractor, the client takes these roles on by default. Note that projects with two or more contractors also trigger the duty to prepare a health and safety file.

The principal designer is the designer with control over the pre-construction phase with emphasis on control over the health and safety elements of the design. Their role will be to plan, manage and monitor compliance with these regulations during the pre-construction phase. Note that the pre-construction phase will include all the time spent planning and preparing for the project before construction starts. The pre-construction phase will also include the designs prepared while construction work is ongoing such as temporary works design, cable-route selection or design and build projects. It follows that the principal designer can change during a project. For example, the architect might be the principal designer before construction starts on site. Then, when a main contractor commences work on site, they may commission their sub-contractors and consultants to prepare detailed designs for the project. The main contractor could then be in control of the remainder of the pre-construction phase and be appointed as the principal designer.

Any company that carries out some design as part of their role could be a principal designer. Note that design includes preparing specifications and bills of quantities as well as the preparation of drawings and calculations. In many cases, the company with the greatest amount of design on a project will be the principal designer, such as the architect for a house extension or a new office block. If there is only one designer for the project, they are most likely to be the principal designer too. However, for a design and build project the principal designer role may move from the architect for the outline design to the main contractor for the project responsible for coordinating the detail design. There are also occasions when the client is best placed to be the principal designer. For example, one of my major clients is a car manufacturing company. Most of the changes made to the factory are linked to the car or cars being manufactured. The factory has a team of designers who don't tend to prepare the detailed designed but who coordinate the efforts of a central design team for the company and the efforts of numerous design and build contractors. They also contribute to the specification and to design changes made on site during the construction phase to achieve the car build-quality required. In this instance, they are the glue that binds the designs from separate designers together and the only people who understand and are aware of the whole design. In this instance, the client's own internal team of designers appears best placed to take on the role of principal designer.

There are those in the construction industry who would tell you that only someone registered and qualified to be a principal designer can take this role on. This is not true. When the regulations changed in 2015, introduction of the '2 or more contractors' threshold for a principal designer meant that a principal designer could be required for a project lasting less than one-working day. What this means is that a proportionate response is required. For most small projects, the only designer or lead designer is usually best placed to take on this role. Naturally, they should make themselves aware of their duties and fulfil them to the best of their ability. It is the client's responsibility to ensure that that they have sufficient skills, knowledge, experience and capability to undertake this role. When doing so, the client should consider the extent of design and its complexity. For many small projects, there is limited design with limited health and safety impact and most competent designers should be able to take on the principal designer role. Of course, you can pay a specialist principal designer to fulfil this role for you. However, it is my experience on small projects, and that of many of my clients, that specialist principal designers rarely understand your business the way that you do and you pay a premium for very little benefit. Conversely, on larger or more complex projects a good, specialist principal designer can add value, especially if you allow them to do their job properly.

The principal contractor is the contractor with control over the construction phase with emphasis on control of health and safety on site. Very often, this will be the main contractor for the project who arranges the site perimeter, the offices, the welfare facilities and who also awards most of the contracts to smaller construction companies. Their role will be to plan, manage and monitor health and safety on site during the construction phase.

The principal contractor may change during a project. For example, a project may have three distinct phases: site investigation, civil & structural, mechanical and electrical. During the site investigation phase there may only be one contractor on site but, because there will be more than one contractor on the project, the site investigation contractor will be the principal contractor for that phase. Their role should be straightforward because they have only to plan, manage and monitor their own work, something they must do anyway as a contractor. When they finish on site, the role of principal contractor defaults back to the client. However, as there is no construction on site, this is just a holding position with almost no responsibility. Then, when the civil and structural stage commences, the main contractor for that phase could be appointed to the role of principal contractor. When the majority of the civil and structural work is complete and the focus moves to the installation of complex mechanical and electrical equipment, such as a production line, the main M&E contractor could be appointed to the role of the principal contractor. The important thing to ensure is that the principal contractor is genuinely in control of health and safety during the construction stage.

If we return to the car manufacturing factory, the client has two options to choose from. If they intend to award a turnkey project where a plot of land or a part of their factory is handed over completely to a main contractor, then it would make sense for the main contractor to be the principal contractor. However, and as happens more frequently, if the client awards lots of contracts itself and controls those contracts as well as organising welfare, regular meetings, permits, access and working time to fit in with car production, it feels as though they are in control of the construction phase. In this situation, the client is probably best placed to be the principal contractor.

In the past, many clients have tried to manipulate compliance with the CDM Regulations by confusing, either through ignorance or deliberate intention, the terms 'contract' and 'project'. The two or more contractor rule applies to the project, not to individual contracts. We explored the definition of project earlier. Another important point to note is that self-employed joiners, electricians and plumbers working on a house extension or a bathroom refurbishment are each classed as a contractor. What these clarifications mean in practice is that very few projects will have only one contractor. Examples might include a brickwork company building a new wall, a fencing contractor erecting a new fence or a media company installing a satellite dish and cable.

Chapter 5 – General Duties
The general duties communicated in regulation 8 apply to all projects and to all duty-holders.

Skills, Knowledge and Experience
Every party with duties under CDM involved in a project, apart from the client, will be a designer or a contractor. Note that the client may even be a designer or a contractor too. Designers and contractors may receive additional duties as a principal designer or principal contractor, but they will still be designers or contractors. The first general duty to apply to designers and contractors is that they must have the skills, knowledge and experience and, if they are an organisation, the organisational capability necessary to fulfil their duties under CDM on their projects. This duty has changed from the 2007 regulations which required all companies to be competent. In practice, this duty has changed very little although the wording used may be more correct.

All companies and self-employed persons in GB are required to understand and to comply with the duties placed upon them by relevant health and safety law. Therefore, it makes sense to check that this is in fact the case. This can be demonstrated by the content of the company health and safety policy and the supporting arrangements. For self-employed persons, this can be demonstrated through interview about their legal duties. This knowledge of health and safety law should be augmented with knowledge of their trade or discipline and the industry sectors in which they work. On a personal level, this knowledge might include knowledge of hazards or techniques relevant to an individual's work. The skills required may range from skills with hand tools and power tools to the skills required to manage large or multi-disciplinary projects. This can be demonstrated through training records or professional qualifications and by evidence of successful completion of previous projects. The experience required can only be demonstrated by involvement in previous projects.

HSE guidance talks about making sensible and proportionate enquiries to determine an organisation's capability to undertake work. For small and low-risk projects, this may mean the use of a shorter or simpler pre-qualification questionnaire. For larger and more complex or high-risk projects, checks may include visiting the company and checking references to determine standards of compliance in practice. The guidance also suggests focussing on the key health and issues rather requiring designers or contractors to jump through hoops for no real benefit. To this end, there is scope for those who engage designers and contractors to make use of standard approaches to determine suitability. One option is to use the standard question set, or a portion of the question set, contained in Publically Available Specification 91 (PAS91). Using the standard questions means that companies can respond quickly and with minimum additional effort by providing their stock responses to standard questions. Also, those engaging designers and contractors could recognise accreditation through SSIP (Safety Schemes in Procurement) affiliated organisations. For example, why ask the same questions as Chas or SafeContractor if a contractor or designer is already accredited with one or both of those schemes. The sensible approach would be to recognise the accreditation already achieved and then focus on any additional questions specific to the proposed design or construction work.

Suitability on paper is only a part of the story. We cannot ignore how a designer or contractor behaves in practice. A prosecution early in 2013 highlights this point. A principal contractor engaged a subcontractor to perform a package of work. On paper, and with standard checks, the subcontractor appeared to be suitable and started work. It soon became clear that they weren't working safely. The principal contractor challenged the subcontractor and provided direction on how to improve. The same pattern was repeated with this subcontractor over several months until one of their workers suffered a fatality. The subcontractor and principal contractor were both prosecuted and the principal contractor was chastised for not removing the subcontractor when it became clear that they were not suitable and were unlikely to become so in good time. This makes it clear that we must judge suitability not just before engagement but during the project. If anyone proves to be unsuitable, they must be challenged, encouraged to improve but, ultimately, if they cannot respond quickly, they must be removed.

It should be noted that no company may accept an engagement or appointment unless they themselves have the necessary skills, knowledge and experience and, if they are an organisation, the necessary organisational capability. Organisations may prove their health and safety compliance levels through accreditation with an SSIP scheme, through external health and safety audits (ISO45001 or British Safety Council Five Star Audit) or they may test themselves against PAS91. The most important thing is for each organisation to be aware of their own limitations and to be careful not to stray beyond them. Limitations may be linked to the size of a project and the organisational capability to manage health and safety for a larger project than is normally undertaken. Limitations may also be linked to the location of a project and the distance from the available resources to support the project. Alternatively, limitations may be linked to the type of work to be undertaken and any activities or industries that fall outside the organisation's normal field of operations. While companies should be encouraged to grow and develop, the increased risks of doing so beyond their normal comfort zones should me met with additional control measures such as buying in expertise or additional monitoring.

Reporting Dangerous Conditions
All individuals involved in construction projects must report any instances that put themselves or others at danger. This could occur during the design stage due to a failure to recognise and manage a problem with an existing structure (lead, asbestos, structural stability) or it could occur during construction (unprotected excavation, lack of vehicle/pedestrian segregation). All individuals should be encouraged and allowed to raise health and safety concerns. Typically, these concerns should be directed to the company or individual with the authority to take the action required. It is equally important that the persons receiving such reports take action to respond to the perceived danger.

Cooperation
All organisations and individuals involved in construction projects must cooperate with all others on the project or with those on an

adjoining site. This will typically involve regular communication, sharing information and looking at the bigger picture rather than being insular. A key activity in cooperation is planning. This enables the organisations working together to look ahead for potential clashes and shared opportunities to manage risk efficiently.

Providing Clear Information or Instruction
A recurring theme within the CDM Regulations is the provision of information or instruction to those who may need it. This is particularly important at the interfaces between the design and construction phases and between separate companies. Health and Safety Executive guidance states that information or instruction should be provided in simple, clear English (and other languages where required), be logical and illustrated where required. Our goal should be to improve the likelihood of information or instruction being understood first time. This challenges the traditional image of contract documents that are so big and complicated that no-one can identify readily what the key health and safety threats might be.

It is also important to note that information and instruction should be provided promptly. For construction projects, important information provided early can save significant amounts of abortive work and increases the likelihood of individuals receiving the information before they are exposed to related hazards. Current technology enables us to collect and store large quantities of information. However, far too often, that information is unavailable because it is buried where only a few can find it or its existence is not known. We should take advantage of information technology to improve the communication of information, but we should also help those involved in projects to identify quickly what information is available and then find and retrieve it efficiently.

Chapter 6 – Clients and Client Duties

Domestic Clients
In chapter 2, we defined the term 'domestic client'. One of the changes introduced by CDM 2015 was to give duties to the client on domestic construction projects. The Health and Safety Executive had resisted this requirement of the European Directive but was forced to make the change in the 2015 regulations. In response, the Health and Safety Executive arranged CDM 2015 to give duties to the 'domestic client' and then promptly pass most of those duties on to someone else. So, how does this work?

Imagine a simple domestic project where the homeowner (the domestic client) wants to form a new patio area and path in their garden. There is very little design involved in this project apart from the sketches prepared by the homeowner. There is only one contractor, the paving company. Therefore, there will be no principal designer or principal contractor. As soon as the paving contractor (the contractor) is engaged to work on the project, he becomes the client. At this point the paving contractor will have all the client duties and all the contractor duties for a project with one contractor. He will relinquish those duties when the project is complete.

Now imagine a slightly bigger project such as building a house extension to build an additional bedroom and en-suite. The homeowner is the 'domestic client'. There will be more than one contractor so this means that there will be a principal designer and a principal contractor. As this project will require planning permission and Building Regulations approval, there will be an architect or building design consultant. They will be a designer. However, as this is a project with two or more contractors, they will also be appointed by the domestic client as the principal designer. At this point, the client can discuss with the principal designer if they are prepared to take on the client role. The principal designer is not obliged to accept this role. Some will see this as a chance to earn additional fees. Others will be alarmed by the potential for additional liability and will shy away from being the client. If the principal designer agrees to taking on the client role it would be a very good idea to record this agreement. However, if the principal designer declines this role, the client role will fall to the principal contractor by default. The principal contractor will be the builder in control of the construction phase.

Once the client role has been passed to another party, the rest of the regulations apply as normal, just with someone other than the 'domestic client' fulfilling the client role.

The Client
The client is usually a company, but it can easily be a partnership, a self-employed person, an association or a charity. It may be that one individual makes all the decisions on behalf of the client, but the client remains the legal entity rather than the individual. It is always a good idea to identify which individual will take the lead when representing the client, even if they rely on other parts of the organisation to execute some client duties. For example, for many larger companies, one Project Manager will be the face of the client when dealing with other parties, but the Procurement Department manages the pre-qualification processes and the Estates Department maintains health and safety file information.

More Than One Client
It is possible for there to be more than one client on any project. For large projects, it is easy to see how this can happen with several project sponsors such as local authorities, utility companies, transport companies and developers all involved in the regeneration of a city centre. Small projects can also have more than one client. Imagine two companies who occupy two halves of an industrial unit. If their roof needs to be repaired or replaced, they may both pay, and both have ideas about how the work should be done.

The CDM Regulations encourage the clients to agree on one of them becoming The Client for their project. This makes life so much easier because there is clarity on who is liable if things go wrong and, therefore, who has the final say about how a project should be managed. While this agreement releases the other potential clients from some client duties, they will still have to cooperate and provide information. They may also have duties as designers for the choices they make. Also, if the work is carried out on their premises, the other clients may have duties under part 4 of the regulations regarding the safety of their existing workplace as it affects contractors.

The alternative, where the clients cannot agree on one lead client, is for all clients to retain their duties with equal liability. This can work well for some duties such as checking designer and contractor suitability and providing information. Where problems arise is when one of the clients appoints either a principal designer or principal contractor or when they disagree on whether a project will have more than one contractor or not. Frankly, this situation should be avoided where possible or there should be a documented agreement explaining how the duties will be executed in practice. The danger with this is that, if something goes wrong, all clients involved could be prosecuted.

A further complication arises when a utilities company is involved in the project. Most requests made to a utilities company (water, electricity, gas etc.) invoke their duties as statutory undertakers. This means that they have a legal obligation to install or divert services and this means that they too are a client. When a domestic customer requests a water meter or a water connection for example, the utility company will become the client as the only contractor involved in the project. However, if a developer wants a new water supply to serve a new housing development there are now two clients involved in the project, the developer and the utility company. The regulations allow for this by permitting the two clients to retain their client duties on the same project or by electing one of them to be the client. It is prudent to record any agreement between the two clients on how they will manage the work under their control. If the amount of work to be undertaken by the utility company is limited, it makes sense to use the developer's principal designer and principal contractor rather than appoint separate ones for the utility company. However, if the utility company needs to lay 2km of water mains for example, it would make more sense to operate as separate projects with separate principal designers and principal contractors. The key to deciding which approach to use is to determine the amount of control each client has over the design and construction of the work packages. Bear in mind though that you cannot subvert the two or more contractors rule by artificially separating the project into several smaller projects.

Arrangements for Managing the Project
The very first duty given to clients in the regulations is to make suitable arrangements for managing a project. Note that this duty applies to projects of all sizes and types. If we swap the word 'plan' for 'arrangement', this may be easier to understand. Every project needs at least one plan, otherwise chaos ensues. For construction projects the plan or plans must ensure that construction work can be carried out safely and that contractors will have decent welfare on site.

In practice, this duty might be achieved as follows. A client wants to build an extension onto their factory. This client already has a health and safety policy and has more detailed procedures for managing health and safety, including one for managing construction projects. As part of the feasibility stage, the client's Project Manager drafts a document called the project management plan which explains the strategy for managing the project. It might include some basic information about the project, the key people involved and gateways or checkpoints at which decisions about the project will be made. The project management plan will be brief at this stage, but we expect it to grow if the project progresses beyond feasibility. It just so happens that the project does progress beyond feasibility and the next stage is initial design and applying for planning permission. The Project Manager reviews the plan and expands it to include items such as budget, approximate programme and who will undertake the outline design for the planning application and who will conduct a desk-top survey to determine the nature of the ground and the presence of utility services. He may also include a quick review of how, if the project goes ahead, welfare facilities would be provided for the expected workforce on site. The plan will evolve further as the project approaches the construction tender stage, construction itself, commissioning and completion.

The client should explain how they will ensure that this project will be a safe and healthy one. The plan should provide clear direction on who is responsible for what. It should explain how sufficient time, space and resources are ensured. It should explain how information will be shared and how frequently designers and contractors will be expected to attend review or progress meetings. The plan should also set out how the client will ensure that the project is safe in practice. This might mean checks on designs or on welfare and security on site. All these actions fulfil the additional duty for the client to ensure that these plans are maintained and reviewed.

Providing Information

Clients must provide information about their structures and projects to designers and contractors who work for them. This makes sense because each client should know more about their existing land, structures and operations than anyone else. Also, the client will have preferences for how the project will be carried out which others may need to know about. This information is known as 'pre-construction information' or PCI. It also makes sense that this information is provided to designers and contractors promptly so that they can consider it in advance of making important decisions.

The regulations recognise that clients may not have all the information that might be needed but dismiss this as an excuse for not providing it. Clients are challenged to determine whether the information needed is reasonably obtainable. For example, the client may have no information on buried services on their land other than there being services somewhere. The presence or absence of services in the location of the proposed structures will have a significant impact on the project. Also, the sooner information on the location and nature of services is known, the smaller the amount of abortive work and impact on the programme. Given that cost-effective techniques are available to locate buried services, the client is duty-bound to provide information about them. The client may choose to arrange surveys himself or he may allow the designer time in the programme and a budget to obtain this information. Either way, the client has ensured that the information is provided.

It would be a mistake to think that providing PCI is something that happens just once. As information becomes available or as the need for a preference or direction from the client becomes apparent, this information should continue to flow. It would also be a mistake to think of PCI as being one document. It is far more useful to think of a folder on a server labelled PCI. This folder would have sub-folders such as project information, management requirements, existing hazards and existing health and safety file information. The information in these folders would grow from next to nothing on day one of the project until just before construction is complete. The client would dip into this folder to extract pertinent information for each designer or contractor and give them the information they need, when they need it. It follows that the designer of the fire alarm system will need very different information to the contractor constructing the foundations, although the basic project description and client preferences for welfare and site rules may be virtually identical.

The HSE guidance provides clear direction on how PCI could be organised and provides direction on what should be communicated, where relevant. The first type of information to be provided is a description of the project. The purpose of this section is clear, to explain to anyone else involved in the project what the scope and purpose of the project is. I find that one effective way to address this heading is to answer a few simple questions. For example: 'What are we building?'; 'Where will it be built?'; 'When will it be built?'; 'Why is it being built?' and; 'Who is involved?'.

The second type of information to be provided is how the client would prefer the project to be planned and managed as well as an indication of the time allowed and the resources required. I find this useful to think of as client preferences. These preferences rarely have an impact on the finished structure, but rather on how the companies involved are expected to behave. It is also useful for establishing responsibility for things such as welfare and security. For example, the client may decide that they want to hold monthly review or progress meetings. They may decide to provide all the welfare themself but let the principal contractor erect and manage the site hoarding. They may choose to impose their permit systems onto all contractors or limit where contractors can go, smoke and park. Each one of these requirements should help the client to protect their own operations and obligations under CDM. For designers and contractors, they can allow for these preferences when pricing for and planning the work. Two preferences or management requirements identified for special attention are the adequacy of time and resources. It is essential that clients are realistic about the amount of time required to design, prepare and to execute construction work and the level of resources required and available for each of these stages. Standards of health and safety on many projects suffer because of unrealistic expectations regarding time or resources. This leads to the cutting of corners and an unhealthy focus on time and money at the expense of health and safety.

The third type of information relates to health and safety hazards on the site or hazards introduced by what has been designed. Think about how well the client knows their own structures and operations. They have a legal obligation to tell others about anything that could have an impact on health and safety while working on their premises. This could include information about the structures such as the presence of asbestos or buried services, previous uses and structural weaknesses. It could also include information about the client's operations such as vehicle movements, high noise levels, substances in the area, explosive atmospheres and levels of dust. Information regarding the hazards involved in design will probably come from the designers themselves to be passed on by the client.

The fourth type of information is any information in an existing health and safety file. This would be information about the structures from a previous project where a health and safety file was prepared. This might include as-installed drawings, load capacities and survey information for asbestos or structural condition.

Note that the amount of PCI should be proportionate to the size of the project, complexity and level of risk. For a project that involves repairing a 1m length of brick wall in the car park after someone backed into it, it would be very difficult to generate more than one or two pages of PCI.

Appointment of a Principal Designer
Only the client can appoint a principal designer and they must do so in writing but only for projects with two or more contractors. This could be achieved as an internal appointment in a procedure or arrangement or as an external appointment via a letter or a record in the minutes of a meeting. The timing of appointment for CDM 2015 appears to be simpler than for the 2007 regulations. In short, if this project is likely to have two or more contractors, and most of them

will, then a principal designer should be appointed as soon as the first designer is engaged and certainly before detailed design commences. In practice, for some clients the initial stages of design start with an internal design process where the bare bones of the design are outlined. In this instance, the client can be the principal designer and, as this role defaults to the client if no appointment is made, this works well. Then, the principal designer role can move to an external designer, if required, as soon as an external designer is engaged.

Where the client has a choice as to who could be the principal designer, they should consider carefully who is most likely to have the greatest control over the design stage of the project. They should also consider whether this role should transfer during the project and how to manage that transfer without the loss of control or information.

Notification
The client is responsible for notifying the project to the enforcing authority if it is a notifiable project. The absolute latest that the project can be notified is the day before any construction commences on the project. This includes notifying before site investigation work commences. In the past, some clients were nervous about notifying too early as this was tied to engaging a CDM coordinator. Now that notification and appointment of a principal designer are completely separate, the client can notify earlier rather than later with no consequences. The most appropriate time to issue the first notification for a project is probably at the beginning of the detailed design stage when most of the information on the notification can be provided.

The easiest way to notify is to use the HSE on-line notification facility. The person who notifies will be given a reference number which enables them to update the notification at any time with very little effort. This means that changes to the key duty-holders can be made whenever they occur.

What do the enforcing authorities do with the notifications? Well, the information is used to help them target their resources towards real projects rather than having to search for projects via other means. This does not mean that projects that are not notified will escape the attention of the enforcing authorities. Inspectors can visit any project at any reasonable time regardless of size or notification.

Appointment of a Principal Contractor

Only the client can appoint a principal contractor and they must do so in writing but only for projects with two or more contractors. Just as for the principal designer, this can be an internal or an external appointment using internal procedures, minutes of meetings or formal letters of appointment. A principal contractor should be appointed before construction work commences on site. The appointment should be made in sufficient time for the principal contractor to prepare the construction phase plan and for subsequent acceptance of the plan by the client. If a project has only one contractor on site to begin with, that contractor is most likely to be the principal contractor. However, the client could appoint a third party to manage the principal contractor duties if they believed this third party would be best placed to do so. This third party could be a contractor with a significant scope of work on the project at a later stage or a construction management company. It is also possible for the client to appoint themselves as the principal contractor if they believe that they have the most control over the management of health and safety on the construction site. Remember that the principal contractor can change during a project and that changes should be communicated in writing.

Construction Phase Plan

The client must ensure that a construction phase plan is in place before construction commences for every project. Note that this duty applies to every project. HSE guidance directs the client to ensure that the construction phase plan adequately addresses the arrangements for managing key risks. The client should also ensure that the principal contractor reviews and updates the construction phase plan. If a client is unfamiliar with construction work or the requirements of CDM, I would always recommend that the client, possibly with support from a construction safety advisor, reviews the construction phase plan and makes comments for improvement before permitting work to commence. It is also advisable to record the fact that the construction phase plan has been reviewed and has been accepted.

Ensuring Compliance

Having appointed a principal designer and a principal contractor, the client must now ensure that they both comply with their duties. This suggests several things. Firstly, it suggests that the client should understand what those duties are. Secondly, it suggests that the client is sufficiently aware of what is happening on their project to be able make a judgement on whether compliance is being achieved. Thirdly, this also suggests that clients can be held accountable in the event of enforcement for allowing a principal designer or principal contractor to behave in a non-compliant manner. This third point emphasises the importance placed on the client role and the impact they can have on the health and safety of a project.

So, how do you ensure that a principal designer and principal contractor are complying with their duties? Typical approaches would be to meet with them regularly and to receive regular reports on progress and performance. The client could also monitor compliance on site from time to time to see what standards of health and safety are achieved by the principal contractor. For larger projects, the client could also arrange audits of the output from designers or the information held by the principal contractor. If the client uses the same principal designers and principal contractors for numerous projects, they could use a process of project review at the end of each project to determine the levels of compliance retrospectively. This can be used to direct improvement for future projects. Note that the efforts made by the client to ensure compliance should be reasonable. This means that they do not have to be exhaustive, but nor should they be cursory or minimal. The question that would be asked in court is what a reasonable client would have done?

Health and Safety File

Health and safety files must be prepared for all projects with two contractors or more. The client is given a new duty in CDM 2015 to ensure that the principal designer prepares a health and safety file for the project. The health and safety file will contain information about the structures built or modified during the project that will be of use when considering health and safety for future projects involving those structures. This new duty emphasises the importance of the health and safety file and that the client should take an interest in it at an early stage in the project.

The client should have an idea of what the health and safety file for the project is likely to contain. They should also have in mind how this information will be stored and retrieved. For example, a client with a relatively small and simple building may prefer to have the health and safety file information in a single hardcopy folder. They may choose to keep the folder in a secure location in the building and bring it out whenever they plan the next construction project.

Another client with several buildings containing different streams of process equipment may choose to use an electronic system in which to store their health and safety file information. They may prefer to store all their drawings in one electronic folder, information about hazardous substances in the structure in another, ground information in another and so on. They would probably have a system for naming and numbering documents and an indexing system to enable them to locate information quickly and easily.

Whichever approach the client prefers, this should be defined in advance and discussed with the principal designer. Then, the client can agree with the principal designer what information is likely to be included and when. This is important because it provides all parties involved with a clear expectation of what the health and safety file should look like at different stages in the project. The client can then measure the actual state of the health and safety file with the expected state at that time.

Another reason for taking an active interest in the development of the health and safety file is that the regulations allow for a change in the principal designer and for responsibility for preparing the health and safety file to move to the principal contractor. It makes sense to insist that a principal designer has completed their portion of the health and safety file before passing it on to another party. Otherwise, that portion may never be completed, or responsibility and ownership could become confused.

The client also has duties towards the health and safety file after the project has finished. They are obliged to revise it to incorporate relevant new information from construction projects and to make it available to those involved in future construction projects. Keeping the health and safety file safe and making it available should be relatively easy to achieve. There is also sound financial sense in holding on to information that has already been paid for that might be needed for the next project and could save the cost of re-surveying.

Keeping the health and safety file up to date could be a far bigger task. For a client with a simple structure with very few changes over the years, this duty might involve limited effort. The client would require the designers and contractors on future projects to provide information for the file and, if the projects involve two or more contractors, the principal designer can use this information to add to or amend the existing health and safety file. In this way, the information in the file should always be accurate and genuinely useful for the next project. Unfortunately, too many clients fail to update their health and safety files.

For clients with larger and more complex health and safety files, they may need a procedure to capture the changes to structures for every project which can then be used to update as-built drawings, service drawings, asbestos registers and manuals stored electronically. For one of my clients with a large factory and countless construction projects, the procedure for projects includes a step to create an electronic folder for every new project. The procedure also includes a step at the end of the project to ensure that all information is filed in the correct sub-folder within the project folder, including as-built drawings. This process can then be audited to ensure that project information is collected and filed correctly. Such a process will incur time, money and effort. The benefit is a level of confidence in the health and safety file information and possible savings in surveys conducted to establish the current structure details. Note that when we use the word 'structure' this also includes cables and pipes and applies to building services as much as it does to the building fabric.

The final duty a client has towards the health and safety file is to pass the health and safety information on to the new owner if they dispose of their interest in the structure. Note that failure to do so could have an impact on the value of the sale in that the new owner may have to pay for surveys to establish information about the existing structure.

Help!

If this is your reaction to the prospect of being a client and all that this role entails, this could well be the right reaction. The client role is a very important one as it sets the tone for the whole project. For clients who regularly undertake construction work this could well be business as usual with established procedures and experienced people to do what needs to be done. They may need very little external help to manage their duties. However, if your construction projects are few and far between, and particularly if they are large or complex, you may need some help. You cannot delegate the liability for your client duties, but you can get help from a construction health and safety specialist. A good construction health and safety advisor will give you several options to choose from. The most expensive option, and possibly the most robust, is to pay a specialist to undertake most of the client functions on your behalf and to act as a project manager. An alternative option is for the specialist to act as a construction health and safety advisor for the project with regular involvement in design stage meetings and on-site inspection. A further alternative is for them to be available at key stages in the project such as project initiation, preparation for tender, commencement on site and project completion. They would also need to be available to provide advice as and when required and to review documents if required.

In my experience, clients who want to do the right thing benefit greatly from the chance to talk through how best to manage their duties with someone who has experience of managing construction health and safety. They help the client to see through the potential complexity of the regulations and to identify specific actions to meet their duties. In these instances, a small investment can often produce significant improvement in the management of projects and can improve peace of mind.

Chapter 7 – Designer Duties

Designers must comply with the general duties discussed earlier as well as the specific designer duties contained in Regulation 9. Remember that designer duties apply to all projects, regardless of size or duration.

Ensuring the Client is Aware of His Duties
Let's assume that the client for a project has never come across the CDM Regulations before. While they are obliged to make themselves aware of any legal obligations they may have for tax, employment law or health and safety, we all know that some still don't have a clue about CDM. So, ask yourself who might be the first professional that the client encounters on a project who does know about CDM. This is often the designer and it is crucial that all designers involved in construction understand the CDM Regulations. Right at the beginning of the project, before any contracts of engagement are signed, the issue of CDM should be raised. I would always minute or record this discussion in some format. It should soon become clear whether the client is or isn't aware of their duties under CDM. If they are aware, then you can carry on with the rest of your duties. However, if they haven't got a clue, the guidance on the HSE website and available from construction skills can be downloaded or printed and shared with the client.

This whole process may cause a little friction with some clients. Some may say that CDM does not apply because theirs is a small project. Feel free to correct them on this and help them to understand the duties that apply to projects with one contractor and with two or more contractors. Other clients may indicate that they have no desire to comply with the CDM Regulations and certainly aren't prepared to pay any extra to do so. For me, this is a wonderful moment on any project. This is one of those light-bulb moments when you see the client's true colours and can predict the nature of your relationship with them on this project. If it is clear the client has no intention of repenting, just walk away. I know that this means losing work but would you rather work for a client who is going to fight you at every step and probably hold back payments or move on to the next job with a client who will work with you? Also ask yourself which project is most likely to have serious accidents and attract the wrong kind of attention from the HSE.

Managing Risk

The crux of a designer's responsibilities under CDM is to eliminate hazards and reduce risks by the choices they make when designing. The priority will always be to try to eliminate hazards where this is reasonably practicable. Let's face it; you can't get safer than no hazard at all. Then, if elimination isn't a sensible option, the designer should reduce the risks from the hazards introduced through his design. The thought process for this will probably include the following steps:

-What existing hazards are there (from the PCI provided by the client or other designers)?
-What hazards have I introduced with the structures I have designed anew or modified?
-Is it reasonably practicable to eliminate any of these hazards with the choices I make?
-Could anyone be affected by these hazards during the construction stage?
-Could anyone be affected by them during modification to the structure or demolition?
-Could anyone be affected by them during cleaning and maintenance of the structure?
-Could anyone be affected by them during use of the structure?
-What options do I have to reduce the risks from any of these hazards at any of these times?
-Which of these options will have the greatest impact at all stages and for all people when reducing risk?
-Select the best options and check what hazards these new options present (repeat some of the above).
-Are there still significant risks left that others need to know about?
-Are any of these significant risks not obvious from the drawings, specification and scope of work or a site visit?
-Make sure that I communicate them clearly so that other people can spot them quickly.

-Has anyone changed anything? (E.g. design during construction) If so, check the above.

For a designer to follow the above process with any success, they need to understand the hazards to which contractors are exposed and the legal requirements imposed on them when managing those hazards. In my experience this means that designers must understand how the structures they design are built. They also need to be sufficiently aware of relevant health and safety legislation so that they can outline the hazards and corresponding control measures. Then, designers should be able to anticipate what will happen in practice and adjust their design so that contractors can comply with the duties imposed on them more readily. The alternative is for contractors to do the best they can despite the design. This often leads to compromise and significant residual risk.

There are limits to every designer's scope of choice when eliminating hazards and reducing risk. For example, if the plot of land for a new structure is limited in size, the designer can't create more space out of nowhere. If the client's budget is limited, the designer's choices for materials and standard of fittings will be limited. Also, if the client is adamant that certain features must be included, the designer may explain the hazards involved in retaining those features but may eventually have to do the best he can with those undesirable features. Think of this as a designer receiving a design brief which includes fixed parameters established by others. The designer may challenge some of those parameters but at some point those parameters will be fixed. The designer cannot be held accountable for the parameters (those were design decisions made by others – such as the client) but he can be held accountable for the choices he makes within those parameters.

Providing Information with the Design
This duty is hugely misunderstood and often poorly executed. In simple terms, designers should communicate information about significant hazards that stem from their design. This information may need to be communicated to other designers, contractors and to the client. In general, if information will be needed after the structure is built; it will probably be needed by the client as part of the health and safety file. If it is needed by other designers who

share design interfaces with you, this will form part of the PCI during the design stage. Note that some of this PCI needed by other designers could well be communicated during design coordination or review meetings. If the information is needed by contractors, this is also PCI but is more likely to be communicated as part of the tender or post tender information.

In the Approved Code of Practice to the 2007 Regulations, the HSE made it perfectly clear that communicating every conceivable hazard from the design stage is pointless. So, don't do it. Most hazards involved in construction are blatantly obvious to competent designers or contractors through a combination of reading the drawings, specification, scope of works and by visiting the site. What designers should focus on is those hazards that aren't obvious or which would have a serious impact if they weren't given sufficient attention. To emphasise this point, consider what happens on far too many projects. Designers finish preparing their design and, just before the tender stage for construction, they prepare some health and safety information with the primary goal of covering their own backsides. They list every hazard they can think of and suggest obvious (and possibly incorrect) control measures such as wearing fall-arrest harnesses and fudge a few numbers on a design risk assessment to make it look as though they have reduced risk. The contractor receives the tender information pack and has only 1 week to plough through it and put a price together. He looks at the health and safety information from the designer. He notices how many pages of information there are and also notices that the information is either blatantly obvious or contains simple or incorrect suggestions for control measures. He decides that his time is better spent looking at the drawings, spec and scope. Unfortunately, there was one useful piece of information buried in the middle of the designer's information that he has now missed and which will cause major problems later on. Does this sound familiar? The problem here is that the designer drowned the contractor in useless information to the point where the few gems of information where hidden from view.

You may have picked up from the above scenario that design risk assessments are a part of the problem. There has never been a requirement for design risk assessments to comply with CDM and far too much time is wasted on them. Don't get me wrong, having a structure to the process of identifying and eliminating hazards and reducing risks is good, as is recording some of your significant findings. This process explains how a designer's choices were influenced and may be useful for reflection by the designer but that isn't what needs to be communicated. In most cases, all that needs to be communicated is what will be built and this is obvious from the drawings, spec and scope. The 'how I decided on this design' information is usually irrelevant. Those who use some form of scoring system for their design risk assessments might also like to consider how irrelevant they are too. Often, a likelihood, severity and risk rating are attached to a hazard before any control measures are selected. This is nonsensical because no construction site I know will have a complete absence of control measures. It appears that the designer is trying to guess what the level of risk would be for a mythical situation. Then, he suggests a few control measures, many of which the contractor would do anyway, and manipulates the severity or likelihood numbers to show how the mythical risk rating has been reduced to a lower level of risk. In practice, the contractor will probably do things very differently to the way the designer envisaged which means that this lower risk rating is just as mythical as the first. What a wonderful use of a designer's time this is.

What is far more productive is to focus on the process of managing risk, as described in the managing risk section above, and to keep a record to ensure nothing is missed. So, the designer lists the hazards he spots from the PCI and his design. They record changes or clarifications to their design, (drawings, spec, scope etc., to eliminate or reduce risks. They identify the residual significant risks and notes where they are made obvious in the drawings, specification and scope of work. If any residual significant risks aren't obvious or need to be emphasised because of their importance, they insert them into drawings, spec, scope of works or a separate document and note where they have been included. What the designer is left with is a register of hazards, controls and where they have been communicated in the PCI which is useful only for themself to check that nothing was missed. The useful information is built into the drawings, specification and scope of work and possibly into an additional document or two.

Non-GB Designers

The nature of construction projects, particularly for process equipment and major projects, is that a proportion of the designers could be based outside Great Britain. To be clear, Great Britain includes England, Scotland and Wales. Technically, the CDM Regulations cannot apply to a designer who operates in Ireland or Spain as they are not at work in Great Britain. Consequently, involving them in any enforcement action becomes complex, expensive and possibly without a meaningful outcome.

The answer to this problem is to place responsibility for ensuring compliance with designer duties with the GB company who engaged the non-GB designer. This makes sense. Presumably, there was some benefit in selecting a non-GB company such as cost saving or specialist knowledge or equipment. Whoever engaged them should consider the potential drawbacks as well as the potential benefits. One of these potential drawbacks is that the non-GB designer may not be aware of the designer duties under CDM and may prepare a non-compliant design. Therefore, the GB company who engaged the non-GB designer should ensure that the design is compliant. This can be achieved using two approaches in tandem. The first is to convert the CDM designer duties into contract terms with the non-GB designer. The second is to conduct at least one review before the non-GB designer's design is released into the project.

Note that if the company who engaged the non-GB designer is also a non-GB company, the client becomes responsible for ensuring that the design is compliant. Consequently, clients need to think carefully before they engage non-GB organisations with direct or indirect design responsibility.

Chapter 8 – Principal Designer Duties

Appointment of the Principal Designer
Remember that every project with two or more contractors must have a principal designer. The guidance document states that the principal designer should be appointed as early as possible in the design process and that this should happen ideally at the concept stage. This means that there is no excuse for not appointing a principal designer early. In practice, during the concept stage of design there will typically be one designer and the scope of design will be very general in nature. Therefore, being a principal designer at this stage should be relatively easy and involve little additional work beyond preparing the concept design. What it should achieve, is questions about the existing structures and pre-construction information being asked early on.

There is some fear among designers about being the principal designer long after their scope of design is finished. The regulations allow for an appointment to have a finite life. For example, an architect could be appointed purely for the planning stage. If planning approval is obtained, the original appointment may come to a natural conclusion and the client may then appoint a new designer to the role of principal designer for the detailed design stage.

The guidance document states that a principal designer is a designer with control over the pre-construction phase of the project. Ideally, this role could be held by one of the parties with a design role in the project rather than a completely independent body with no design function. However, clarification provided by the HSE and the Association for Project Safety indicates that the principal designer need not have any direct design scope on the project in order to be appointed.

Plan, Manage and Monitor
The core function of the principal designer is to plan, manage and monitor the pre-construction phase and to coordinate matters relating to health and safety. The aim of this function is to ensure that the project is carried out without risk to health or safety. All principal

designers would do well to remember this aim. Anything that doesn't achieve it, probably won't add value and may distract from it.

If we break down the three core functions, we see that the first one is to plan. Principal designers must understand the design process and the nature of the structures that will be constructed as part of the project. They must think ahead to identify the steps that the design team will go through and the information required and the decisions to be taken with each step. While other parties may be deeply engrossed in the design problem on their desk now, the principal designer must be able to see what is coming and make plans to ensure that the design team is prepared. Note that the principal designer may need to document arrangements in order to explain their plan for managing the pre-construction phase. This should include evaluating the time required for each stage of a project.

The second function is to manage. This means applying the plans made earlier in a consistent manner or, put more simply, 'doing what we said we would'. To manage, a principal designer must be present and involved in the project often enough to be able to manage health and safety during the pre-construction phase. One advantage of having the principal designer as a designer already involved in the project is that they can be involved and aware of the design progression as an integral part of their role. It is hoped that this will offer an improvement over some CDM coordinators who were too remote from projects and unaware of what was actually happening during the design stage. Another interesting benefit of the principal designer being the designer in control of the pre-construction phase is that they may well be responsible for engaging some of the specialist designers involved in the project. This means that their health and safety responsibility and their contractual authority should align. This should give principal designers the authority that was lacking for many CDM coordinators.

The third function is to monitor. This means measuring performance of health and safety management during the pre-construction phase and acting where performance falls short of the required levels. The things to be monitored during the pre-construction phase may include:

- The provision of relevant pre-construction information
- The quality of pre-construction information
- Attendance at meetings designed to aid cooperation and information sharing
- Information provided for the health and safety file
- The extent to which designers eliminate hazards and reduce risks
- The quality of information provided by designers for use by other parties
- The overall skills, knowledge and experience demonstrated by designers

Identify, Eliminate or Control Risks
There appears to be duplication in this role. We noted earlier that every designer must identify and eliminate hazards and then reduce the level of remaining risks. In practice, designers are still expected to do this and there is no expectation that the principal designer should repeat this process for every hazard. What is more likely is that the principal designer will ensure that each designer is eliminating hazards and reducing risks within their scope. They may focus on the key hazards for a project and work with designers to ensure that these are managed effectively. Where principal designers can certainly add value is by considering the hazards that affect the wider project rather than one particular designer's scope. Examples might include the layout of the construction site and space around the proposed structures, traffic management issues or responding to hazards from neighbouring structures or activities. Using this layered approach, detail design hazards by the designers and strategic hazards by the principal designers, should ensure that hazards at all levels are identified and managed. Note that this process will apply to hazards in construction (initial, subsequent modification and deconstruction), maintenance, cleaning and use of a structure.

Ensuring that Designers Comply
This duty links with the duty to monitor the pre-construction phase. Designers should expect a principal designer to meet with them and to understand how they achieve compliance. The principal designer may check that the team assigned to the project has the skills, knowledge and experience required for their scope. They may also review the output from designs, including the timeliness of provision

and the quality of the information. In particular, given that principal designers are responsible for collating the health and safety file, they should take an active interest in the provision of health and safety file information by designers as it becomes available. It follows that the principal designer should take corrective action, either directly or with the support of the client, where designers fail to comply with their duties.

The principal designer is specifically tasked with ensuring that all parties involved in the pre-construction phase cooperate with each other. This paints a picture of the principal designer as an enabler or facilitator. You would expect a principal designer to have an overview of the pre-construction phase which allows them to identify which parties need to cooperate in order to manage risk. In practical terms this will mean directing parties to work together and ensuring that project meetings are organised, attended and used to good effect.

Assisting the Client
There is a definite change here from the role of the CDM coordinator. CDM 2015 directs the principal designer to assist the client only with regard to pre-construction information. If the client requires assistance with his other duties, it is expected that he will arrange for such competent assistance in line with existing duties under Regulation 7 of the Management of Health and Safety at Work Regulations.

The principal designer should work with the client to check the pre-construction information that the client has already compiled. Note that clients are supposed to make some effort to identify any existing information they have that may be relevant or to commission surveys or studies to obtain information that can reasonably be obtained. The principal designer may identify errors, contradictions or gaps in this information and then identify to the client further pre-construction information to be provided. The key duty to provide further pre-construction information remains with the client but the principal designer should assist the client to the extent that this is within his control. Similarly, to the extent of his control, the principal designer should provide pre-construction information to designers and contractors involved in the project.

In practice, it would be a mistake to think that every document must pass through the principal designer's hands. However, you would expect them to have a good grasp of the information that is available, has been provided, is needed and who either needs it or will provide it. This can't happen unless the principal designer has sufficient involvement in the project.

The principal designer may advise the client on tools or techniques to achieve effective information management. This might include tools such as distribution lists or transmittal notes and good version control and labelling. It may include the use of sharing systems such as Google Drive, SharePoint, Drop Box or similar. It should also involve meetings, particularly among designers, to achieve a certain quality of information communication.

Liaison with the Principal Contractor
There are two key reasons why the principal designer should liaise with the principal contractor. The first is to ensure that the principal contractor has the information needed to prepare a relevant and useful construction phase plan. This is often achieved as part of, or shortly after, a contract award meeting. Then, we must recognise that the pre-construction phase will almost always continue well into the construction phase. The principal designer will need access to the designers involved in the construction phase to ensure compliance and facilitate cooperation. This will include contractors with detailed design within their scope and also with temporary works designers.

Where a project has a significant amount of design and build, there is a strong argument for the main contractor to be appointed as the principal designer as well as being the principal contractor. Note that the principal designer should be the designer in control of the pre-construction phase. This allows for the principal designer to change to reflect a change in who is genuinely in control at any point in the project.

Health and Safety File
The principal designer has two clear responsibilities towards the health and safety file: to prepare it and then to issue it to the client at the end of the project. A good principal designer will, at the beginning of the project, set out the likely structure and content of

the health and safety file and agree this with the client. This means that, as part of the pre-construction information, the preferred format should be known by all those contributing, and the principal designer should know who will provide which information. Note that very little of the health and safety file is actually written by the principal designer. Their role in preparing it should be to collate information prepared by others and then provide the glue that binds it all together. There is no reason why the principal contractor cannot do some of the collation and quality checking for the information stemming from his construction team and in practice this happens most of the time. The danger with this approach is to remember that not all the information for the health and safety file will be created by the construction team. What about information generated by the client (asbestos surveys) and designers (maximum loadings, deconstruction sequences)? How would the principal contractor know about and collate such information?

If you imagine a principal designer's desk at the point where he is about to compile the health and safety file, their role in its compilation becomes clearer. There will be information from numerous sources of varying quality and adherence to the preferred format and structure. Can you envisage that there will be gaps in this information, duplication of information and contradictory information? Now you can see that the principal designer's role is to take what could easily be a disparate collection of random information and turn it into a genuinely useful resource for future construction safety involving the structures built or modified as part of this project.

A trick that I learned a while ago is to create a draft folder structure for the health and safety file in a folder on the server. The folder structure is organised in the manner preferred by the client or suggested by me and adopted by the client. The sub-folders might be organised by discipline or structure or type of information (historical surveys, asbestos information). Within each sub-folder is a Word document setting out what I believe the contents for that folder will be (and later what they actually are). I also prepare a master health and safety file document listing all the expected information in broad terms, not specific documents, who will provide it and when in the project I would expect it to be provided.

For example, if an asbestos survey is prepared for a structure and the intention is to leave the asbestos containing materials untouched, I know that I can incorporate the survey into the health and safety file, along with the asbestos management plan, shortly after the survey is produced during the initial design stage. Later, if the structure has a steel frame, I know that the as-built drawings for the steel frame should be complete approximately 2 weeks after the steel frame is installed and signed off. So, I communicate this to the steel structure contractor and the Quantity Surveyor so that recognition of his completion of the work is tied in with provision of those drawings. What this means is that the health and safety file is collated gradually so that by the time the project actually ends on site, the only information outstanding should relate to finishes.

Once complete, the task of passing the health and safety file onto the client seems an easy one. However, it would be a mistake to hand the file to the client, along with the final invoice, and walk away. It is crucial that the client is shown how the health and safety file works, how to find information, how to update it and just how useful the contents will be for future construction projects. Then, with a bit of luck, there is a chance that they will actually make use of it.

There is an important change in CDM 2015 to the way that health and safety files are prepared. The regulations now allow for the situation where the principal designer's involvement in the project finishes before the end of the project. In such situations, the principal designer must pass the health and safety file on to the principal contractor. This change emphasises the point that the health and safety file should be collated as the project progresses. Information generated prior to tender that is relevant to the health and safety file should be captured and organised in the health and safety file either at the same time or shortly afterwards. Information from the construction team should be available no more than a few weeks after an element of the structure is mechanically complete. What must not happen is for the principal designer's role in the project to end and for the principal contractor to be handed a health and safety file which has significant gaps for information that should have been captured already. Note that there is a clear client responsibility to ensure that the principal designer prepares the health and safety file. Consequently, it follows that if the client allows the principal designer's involvement to finish before the end of the project, he must check that the file is as complete as it can be when it is handed to the principal contractor.

Projects with One Designer

Now that CDM2015 requires principal designers for projects with just two contractors, it is far more likely that many small projects will have a principal designer as the only designer involved in the project. In such a situation the duty to ensure that designers comply with their duties is limited to self-checking. The duty to ensure cooperation is also easier as the number of parties will be far smaller. The duties relating to assisting the client with pre-construction information and preparation of the health and safety file remain. It could be argued that the client may need more assistance with the pre-construction information on such projects as clients with smaller projects may be less experienced in managing their CDM duties. On smaller projects the budget for the principal designer is likely to be limited. Therefore, on such projects, the principal designer's role is more likely to finish long before the end of the project. This means that the principal designer will need to do as much work as possible in setting up the structure of the health and safety file and then leave the principal contractor with clear instructions on how to populate it.

Domestic Projects

Remember that, on domestic projects, the client is most likely to be the only contractor on the project or the principal contractor. This means that, instead of dealing with the domestic client, the principal designer must treat the contractor or principal contractor as the client for the project. Therefore, this means assisting them to obtain and provide pre-construction information as well as providing them with the health and safety file either at the end of the project or when their role finishes in their role.

There is a genuine concern that many house extension designers are unprepared for CDM 2015 and the impact it will have on their role. It is crucial that these designers understand their duties as a designer and principal designer and then use a proportional approach to discharge those duties properly. This needn't be complicated, but it will require a little more effort and time than was required

previously. Key things to ensure will be:
- Early identification of who the client is for the project.
- Ensuring that the client is aware of their duties.
- Agreeing the point at which the principal designer's role will finish
- Identifying pre-construction information already provided and required.
- Ensuring that information about asbestos containing materials and buried services is provided.
- Identifying any other companies with design responsibility and working with them.
- Starting the health and safety file (structure and expected contents).
- Inserting information into the health and safety file as it becomes available.
- Agreeing with the principal contractor who will generate the as-built drawings.
- Passing the health and safety file on to the principal contractor when the principal designer role finishes or at the end of the project.

Chapter 9 – Contractor Duties

Contractors have duties on all construction projects. Some will only apply on projects with two or more contractors. However, most contractor duties apply to all contractors on all projects. Also remember that every principal contractor is also a contractor and must comply with these duties too.

The contractor duties will apply to anyone carrying out construction work as part of their business, including the principal contractor. Note that this excludes a homeowner carrying out DIY. If you recall the definition of 'construction work' it should be apparent that these duties will apply to a large number of companies and self-employed persons involved in everything from building skyscrapers to installing a satellite dish to a home. These duties apply to contractors working for domestic clients in the same way as for a commercial or industrial client. The same is true for the general duties covered earlier in this book. The only difference is that, on projects for domestic clients, the contractor, or principal contractor, will also receive and be expected to carry out the duties of the client for the project.

Is the Client Aware?
The first of the contractor duties is another gateway or checkpoint and relates to the client's awareness of his own duties under CDM. Let's assume that a client wants to strip out the internals from a factory building. There is no design and no designers have been engaged. So, the first construction professional engaged by the client is a contractor. This is the first chance that anyone involved in construction has to check whether the client knows anything about CDM. As part of the initial discussions about the proposed work, the contractor should ask if the client is aware of his duties. Either the client will be aware and the project can move on to the next step or he won't be aware and the contractor can issue the client with the HSE's guidance for clients. This should make life easier when it comes to the client providing information about the existing structures and allowing for decent welfare facilities. If the client is not aware of their duties under CDM, no construction work may be

carried out until this is rectified. On domestic projects, the contractor will become the client and they must, therefore, understand the client duties themself before they can commence construction work.

Plan, Manage and Monitor

Contractors must plan, manage and monitor construction work they carry out and work carried out by their subcontractors. In truth, this duty exists already in the Management of Health and Safety at Work Regulations but is communicated more succinctly here. This duty is the core responsibility that contractors have and focuses on three important words: plan; manage and; monitor. Planning suggests that each contractor anticipates the health and safety issues associated with their proposed work and identifies appropriate control measures. Then the contractor communicates and applies those control measures i.e. they manage them. Finally, they observe levels of compliance, health and safety and use this information to improve. This is the Plan-Do-Check-Act cycle. It is particularly important to note that this applies not just to the work carried out by the contractor but also any work carried out by others under their control. This contradicts the widely held perception that subcontracting work means subcontracting responsibility too. Any contractor who does subcontract work must ensure that they plan, manage and monitor that work so that they and their subcontractor(s) coordinate and execute their work without risk to health and safety. It follows that unsafe work by a subcontractor would warrant corrective action by the contractor and that this chain of responsibility exists regardless of how many subcontract relationships there may be.

Time, Information and Instruction

Contractors must ensure that there will be enough time to carry out the proposed work. This includes ensuring that every subcontractor has enough time to consider the pre-construction information, the scope of works, prepare their plans and communicate them in readiness to start work on site. Contractors must also provide every construction worker under their control with information they need to work safely. This will typically include a suitable induction, information on risks and control measures (usually in a method statement or daily briefing), site rules and details of emergency procedures. Note that this will apply regardless of the size or nature of project. For the smaller or simpler sites, this might be a brief induction with regular ongoing communication from the person managing the construction work.

Appropriate Supervision
A clarification introduced in CDM 2015 is the duty to provide appropriate supervision in addition to information and instruction. This duty is already present in the Management of Health and Safety at Work Regulations but is repeated here for emphasis. In practice, contractors have a choice to make in order to comply with this requirement. They can ensure that a supervisor visits each gang with sufficient regularity to ensure that they rarely stray from the planned safe methods of work. If this is not practicable and gangs have to operate remotely, each gang should have its own working supervisor who is trained and sufficiently experienced to fulfil a supervisory role. We know from experience that allowing gangs to work without any supervision will, in many cases, lead to deviation and unsafe work practices.

Skills, Knowledge, Training and Experience
Contractors must not employ a person to work on a construction site unless that person has, or is in the process of obtaining, the skills, knowledge, training and experience required to carry out the tasks allocated to them. Once again, this general requirement is already set out in the Management of Health and Safety at Work Regulations. For work on construction sites there are two elements to the skills, knowledge, training and experience required. The first relates to the individual's trade. The employer must ensure that any tradesman is capable of using the work equipment, work techniques and substances required by their trade. They should also be able to anticipate the hazards inherent in their trade activities and to recall suitable control measures. The second element relates to work on construction sites in general. This requires all those who work on construction sites to have a general awareness of the hazards present on construction sites and the general control measures required to work safely on and around them. This is what the CSCS card scheme aims to demonstrate with a trade qualification as well as completion of a general health and safety test. Note that this is not the only way to demonstrate compliance.

Security and Welfare

Then there are two requirements that prevent a contractor from working unless things are in place, specifically security measures and welfare facilities. So, regardless of the size or nature of a construction site, there must be the means to prevent unauthorised access. This might vary from an individual standing in a corridor asking people to wait through to 2.4m high hoarding and 24-hour security. The important thing to note here is that unauthorised persons can't just wander into the area where construction work is underway. The second requirement is to ensure that suitable welfare facilities are provided throughout the construction phase. For the smallest domestic project, you would expect the builder and client to come to an agreement so that the builder's workers can use the downstairs toilet and washbasin, plug their kettle in and have somewhere to shelter. They usually sit in their van to eat their lunch and, while this is not perfect, it does allow them to rest in relative comfort. Note that all welfare facilities (vans included) must be kept reasonably clean. The fact that the requirement for welfare facilities applies to domestic projects too explains why we see more and more portable toilets in front of house extensions.

On larger projects there are several possible providers of the welfare facilities. The client might provide all the welfare or the principal contractor or each of the contractors might be required to provide their own. Alternatively, one party might provide communal toilet and washing facilities and leave each contractor to provide their own changing, drying, eating, rest and drink facilities. These facilities must be maintained throughout the project and must adjust to remain suitable for the size of the workforce and their welfare needs. If the welfare facilities are provided by others, any contractor who relies on them should check that they are suitable. If not, it follows that they must bring it to the attention of the provider and require improvement. In extreme cases of poor welfare, I have known contractors bring in additional welfare facilities and claim, legitimately, for a variation to the contract.

Construction Phase Plan

Note that construction phase plans are required for all construction projects. This means that a contractor working alone on a project must develop and implement a suitable construction phase plan.

This needn't be complicated or time consuming. In fact, the template for a simple construction phase plan available on the HSE website and the phone app available from the same location should make it very easy for a small contractor to prepare a basic plan. It is hoped that the use of these plans will serve to educate those contractors less familiar with health and safety law in some of the key construction safety control measures. In practice, most projects with only one contractor are likely to be shorter in duration. Therefore, there may be no real need to review and update the construction phase plan. However, it is possible to have a project with one contractor and a long construction period. In this instance, the contractor should definitely review and update the plan.

For projects with more than one contractor the principal contractor must, before construction starts on site, prepare a suitable construction phase plan so that the initial phase of work on site can be planned, managed and monitored effectively. Then, the principal contractor must communicate and implement the construction phase plan to enable compliance. They must also review, revise and refine it so that it remains relevant for the impending construction activities and nature of the changing site. The construction phase plan is meant to be a genuinely useful document to the principal contractor and contractors. For the principal contractor it provides a manual to explain how to run the project on site safely. For contractors, it helps them to price for their responsibilities and plan their activities and personnel to comply with the principal contractor's expectations.

The HSE guidance document L153 provides clear direction on the sort of information that a construction phase plan might contain. I find it useful to bear a few questions in mind when preparing and reviewing construction phase plans. Firstly, to be relevant to this project, does it take account of the pre-construction information? Secondly, does it communicate to the wider construction team the information that they need to know? Thirdly, if I was the Site Manager, would the information it contains actually help me to manage health and safety on the project? If the answer to any of these questions is 'No', I suggest trying again.

Note that the construction phase plan should be seen in context with other documents. For example, you would not expect to see a health and safety policy or company health and safety procedures in a construction phase plan. These documents, which form part of a company's safety management system, should exist at a level above the construction phase plan and may, in fact, mention the fact that construction phase plans will be developed for projects. Then, the construction phase plan will explain how contractor risk assessments and methods statements will be reviewed and how information for the health and safety file will be reviewed. Note that the plan should not contain the method statements and risk assessments because these documents exist at a level below the construction phase plan. The construction phase plan should explain the strategy for managing health and safety and the method statements should contain the detail of hazards and control measures for specific activities.

Working with the Principal Designer and Principal Contractor
For projects with two or more contractors, contractors are required to follow the directions of the principal designer and the principal contractor. The principal designer is charged with responsibility for pre-construction but also for preparing the health and safety file. If a contractor has design elements within their scope, they must already cooperate with the principal designer as a designer. So, it appears that this duty relates to the need to provide information for the health and safety file. In simple terms, if the principal designer asks for information from a contractor for the health and safety file, the contractor must provide it in good time and to a reasonable standard.

Contractors are also required to comply with the directions of the principal contractor and to comply with relevant parts of the construction phase plan. It follows that the principal contractor must have communicated the plan to the contractors at some point for this to happen. When it comes to complying with the principal contractor's directions this is very important. The principal contractor bears a great deal of responsibility on construction sites for standards of health and safety. A good principal contractor will monitor health and safety compliance by contractors and will provide direction to correct unsafe work or deviation from approved safe methods of work. Contractors must recognise the authority given to principal contractors in managing health and safety on site and, therefore, must comply. Clearly, if what the principal contractor has directed a contractor to do is unsafe or manifestly wrong, this should be discussed further before taking any action. If there is still disagreement, the matter should be referred upwards to line managers rather than working unsafely.

Chapter 10 – Principal Contractor Duties

Principal contractor is a term defined in the CDM Regulations and applies to projects with two or more contractors only. Note that principal contractor and main contractor are often confused. Main contractor is a contract law term for the contractor to whom the major work packages are awarded and who then subcontracts to other contractors. On many projects the principal contractor is also likely to be the main contractor.

Construction Phase Plan
On projects with two or more contractors, the principal contractor is responsible for preparing, issuing, reviewing and implementing the construction phase plan. The construction phase plan was explored in some detail in the previous chapter.

Managing Health and Safety on Site
With the construction phase plan written, the principal contractor now has a structure within which to plan, manage and monitor health and safety on site. The fact that a principal contractor must fulfil these three general responsibilities hints strongly that the principal contractor should be on site in order to do so. For a single-location project, it would make sense for the principal contractor to be on site almost all of the time. For multi-location sites, being on each site almost every day for a suitable period of time would seem appropriate. This is reinforced by duties to ensure compliance with relevant legislation and with the construction phase plan. Ask yourself how a principal contractor can do this if they are not present?

Much of what a principal contractor must do involves communication and organisation. They must communicate relevant sections of the construction phase plan to contractors, this would include the site rules. They must organise cooperation among the contractors on site. This cannot happen without an effective two-way communication process. A key element of this coordination is being fully aware of who will be working where, when and how. One practical way to achieve this is to develop a week-by-week plan of activities. This can be discussed in advance to highlight potential high-risk activities, clashes and logistical arrangements. Done properly, all contractors on the project will welcome this process and the chance to reduce the number of surprises and lost hours of work.

All workers must receive a suitable site induction. There is flexibility in who provides this, but the principal contractor must ensure that it is provided. The principal contractor also has similar duties to those of all contractors to prevent unauthorised access and to ensure that suitable welfare facilities are maintained throughout the project. In practice, you would expect the principal contractor to have a major role in ensuring a secure site and this ties in with the duty that each contractor has to check that this is the case before they are allowed to start work. The duty to ensure suitable welfare does not require the principal contractor to provide it, only to ensure that, whoever provides it, it is always suitable. This suggests that the principal contractor should check on levels of provision and the quality of provision. For example, if the client undertakes to provide and maintain all welfare facilities but isn't cleaning them well enough, the principal contractor should bring this to the client's attention and expect an improvement. Similarly, if contractors provide their own welfare cabins, you should expect the principal contractor to inspect them from time to time and require improvements where warranted.

One duty stands alone from the others in that it relates to the duty to cooperate with the principal designer with regard to the pre-construction phase. This is the reciprocal duty imposed on the principal designer and creates a clear relationship in order to ensure that designs prepared during construction are treated in a similar way to those undertaken during the design period. Note that the pre-construction phase can run concurrently with the construction phase until all elements of design, including temporary works design, are complete.

Complying with Health and Safety Law
The principal contractor is charged with coordinating implementation of applicable legal requirements for health and safety by the contractors working on the project. This means that the principal contractor must ensure that contractors comply with

current, relevant health and safety legislation. Now, each contractor, as an employer in their own right, has the duty to comply with relevant health and safety legislation. As we know, that doesn't necessarily mean that they will comply on every occasion. So, it appears that the principal contractor is required to be aware of the relevant health and safety legislation for all construction work planned on the project and to then ensure that it is complied with by all contractors. The inference is that if a contractor fails to comply with the health and safety law on site, the principal contractor allowed that to happen. Therefore, as well as the contractor being liable for enforcement action, the principal contractor may also be liable. This may seem harsh. However, this is the nature of the principal contractor role and it explains why the principal contractor needs to plan, manage and monitor health and safety matters robustly to ensure, so far as is reasonably practicable, that all contractors comply with their legal duties. This also means that the individuals responsible for execution of the principal contractor role need to have a good grasp of relevant health and safety legislation. This might suggest completion of the Site Manager's Safety Training Scheme course. On larger or more complex sites, this could suggest completion of the Nebosh Construction Certificate or equivalent.

The principal contractor is also required to ensure that contractors apply the principles of prevention in a consistent manner and that they comply with the construction phase plan. If the construction phase plan has been written to comply with relevant legislation and to meet the specific needs of the project and the existing site, then this duty will be very similar to the one described in the paragraph above. In practical terms, the principal contractor can achieve compliance through planning, method statement review, regular monitoring and redirection.

The planning element involves looking ahead to the activities due to happen in the coming weeks. The principal contractor should be able to identify the legislation that will apply to those activities and consider both at an individual contractor level and at a site level what control measures will be required. Then, the principal contractor will need to review the method statements for the proposed work. Here is where a principal contractor can add real value. The method statements must be presented sufficiently far in advance to allow for a genuine review and a chance to change the method and/or the equipment and people before work starts. The principal contractor should then ask the following questions: 'How?', 'With what?' and 'What if it goes wrong?' for each of the activities described in the method statement. If the answers to these questions aren't clear from the method statement, more information is required. Once the answers are clear, the principal contractor will need to determine if what they describe complies with relevant legislation. The output from this process should be good, clear method statements that will be useful to the principal contractor, the contractor's supervision team and even to the individual workers. Now we come to regular monitoring. Knowing the planned work and the intended method, the principal contractor can talk through the intended method with those responsible on the day and then observe construction activities as they happen. If the method statement is followed and compliance is demonstrated, this provides an opportunity to offer praise or thanks for a job well done. If non-compliance is observed, it should be corrected at the earliest opportunity and recorded.

Recording and Learning from Compliance Levels
In traditional accident triangle theory, there is a statistical probability that a company will have a certain number of fatalities, major injuries, minor injuries and damage events for a given number of working hours. This could be calculated from national or company statistics. You would expect minor injuries to occur more frequently than major injuries and major injuries to occur more frequently than fatalities and so on. However, this theory assumes that you do nothing to learn from your damage events and minor injuries to reduce the likelihood of more serious events. To start reducing the likelihood of negative incidents, the first step is to report all such incidents, to investigate the causes and to address the causes to reduce the likelihood of a recurrence. However, there will come a point where the number of negative incidents ceases to provide sufficient opportunities for improvement. This is where a company needs to identify near-miss events but also to identify unsafe acts and unsafe conditions. A good principal contractor will observe levels of compliance and will identify, record, rectify and report on

non-compliance, unsafe acts and unsafe conditions. What this does is to capture the causes of incidents before they have a chance to become a negative incident. The causes may be procedural, material (equipment or substances) or behavioural in nature and the intention with this approach is to change procedures, material and behaviour through regular attention and correction. In time, the principal contractor can also introduce a system for identifying, recording and reporting on good practice to recognise the kind of practices that are most desirable on sites.

Not only is the approach described above an effective way to reduce the likelihood of negative incidents and to improve compliance, it also offers the principal contractor a lot of protection. Using this approach, a principal contractor can demonstrate with recorded evidence that they regularly monitor contractor work, that non-compliance is detected and rectified and that improvement in compliance levels is achieved. In the event of a serious accident, the principal contractor could turn to this evidence as proof of complying with their legal duties. In particular, they can demonstrate that they did everything reasonably practicable to ensure legal compliance. Without this kind of evidence, how would you demonstrate that you ensured compliance to the Health and Safety Executive or to a Civil Court.

Consultation with the Workforce
For employees working in an office or factory the legislation for union and non-union consultation is well defined and should be easy to implement. However, for construction workers who might work on a different site every one or two months, this can be much harder to achieve. So, the principal contractor is directed to make and implement arrangements to achieve consultation with the workforce in addition to any consultation arrangements in place with their employers. This consultation would typically relate to site-specific issues such as site rules, welfare facilities and improvement initiatives. Similarly, the principal contractor is directed to make health and safety information available to workers or their representatives relevant to their health and safety. This might facilitate the duties that safety representatives or representatives of employee safety may have towards fellow workers. Note that any sensitive information, such as commercially sensitive information or

information covered under the data protection act does not have to be made available.

In practice, the way in which consultation is achieved will be appropriate to the size of the project, the number of workers, the project length and the typical workforce turnover. The most common format on large projects is to establish a worker forum separate from supervisor meetings. Note that this forum will need clear direction on what their purpose is and what topics fall into their scope.

The regulations require the principal contractor to make and maintain arrangements which will enable the principal contractor and workers to cooperate effectively in developing, promoting and checking the effectiveness of health, safety and welfare measures. This can be summarised as 'worker engagement'. While there are still examples of old-style dictatorial construction sites, there are also increasing number of projects where workers are able to contribute to health, safety and welfare issues. Construction workers are likely to have worked on many construction sites, often a wider range of sites than those who manage them. It follows that they will have experienced both good and bad sites in terms of standards of health, safety and welfare and ways of managing projects. Worker engagement can be achieved using simple suggestion schemes, daily briefings with a slot for feedback or questions and information boards with 'You said, we did' sections. These boards often identify insightful observations made by workers and corresponding action by site managers. Once workers realise that their observations, concerns or complaints are received and acted upon, this often encourages more of the same with genuine improvement in health, safety and welfare.

Chapter 11 – Health and Safety on Construction Sites

While parts 1 and 5 of CDM deal with admin and parts 2 and 3 deal with how construction projects should be managed, part 4 provides direction on practical health and safety on site. Much of what we see in part 4 is very similar to the former Construction (Health, Safety and Welfare) Regulations. Part 4 of CDM applies to all construction projects and to all persons who either carry out construction work or control the way in which construction work is carried out. It is obvious that this includes principal contractors and contractors. What isn't immediately obvious is that this could also include the client and managing agents. For example, the local water company has a water treatment works. This water treatment works has a road system, external and internal lighting, buildings with fire alarm systems and guardrails around tanks containing water. If the water company asks a contractor to work on site, the contractor cannot suddenly become responsible for the traffic management system, the existing guardrails or the fire detection systems. These will remain in the water company's control and should protect the contractor. If, however, the contractor is tasked with removing a guardrail, then you would expect them to take responsibility for edge protection in that specific location.

Rather than summarise the whole of the regulations here, I would direct you to look at the headings of the regulations in part 4. For most of the headings, the expectations are obvious and there are well established control measures on most construction sites. However, a few points warrant special mention.

Good Order
I particularly like the requirement for every part of a construction site to be kept in good order and in a reasonable state of cleanliness. The phrase 'good order' invokes images of organisation, tidiness and everything where it should be. You can apply 'good order' to a desk, to a van, the inside of an excavator and even to the kitchen facility on site. Good order suggests that someone owns the area and is responsible for keeping it in a safe and organised condition. A

useful tip for achieving this is to have clear allocation of areas of control and to use a form of demarcation to mark one area of the site from the next. When managing construction safety at an automotive plant we insisted that every contractor defined their work area and placed their company name and contact details on the demarcation. They were then held accountable for the state of that work area.

Stability of Structures

Structures are at their least stable when they are being built, being modified and being deconstructed. We are required to ensure that they remain stable, even during these periods by using temporary supports and limiting the imposed loads. Many companies use temporary works coordinators to support this requirement and it also makes sense to liaise with the principal designer, especially where the stability of existing structures is concerned. It is worth noting that the HSE has used this requirement as the basis for prosecution concerning scaffold collapse incidents. On most occasions, the collapse is caused by insufficient ties to the structure either with or without sheeting fixed to the face of the scaffold.

Energy Distribution Installations

This duty is really just the embodiment of HSE guidance documents HSG47 for underground services and GS6 for overhead services. It applies to all services where energy is conveyed and includes power cables, gas mains, fuel lines and high-pressure mains. Think of it this way, if you hit any of these with a jackhammer, there would be serious consequences. So, we are given a hierarchy to follow by avoiding the services, diverting them, isolating them or protecting them in some other way.

Emergency Procedures

It should go without saying that every construction site should have emergency procedures of some description. Examples that would apply to all sites might include a fire evacuation plan and a first-aid plan. Emergencies mentioned in other regulations are relevant here such as those for escape and rescue from confined spaces and rescue from work at height equipment such as fall-arrest harnesses or cherry-pickers. Other emergencies may need an emergency response plan such as flooding, structural instability, release of a substance, overturning of plant, road-traffic accident or a person falling into a water tank. Some of these emergency procedures will apply to all persons on site while others may apply only to gangs carrying out particular tasks. Some may be existing arrangements generated by the client while many will be developed by the principal contractor or contractors. It is vital that these arrangements are documented and communicated to those people who may need to apply or manage them. This is where many companies stop but, in doing so, they fail to comply with an important step in managing emergency preparedness. The regulations also demand that emergency procedures are tested at suitable intervals. This is crucial because we rely on emergency procedures as the means for safeguarding life in foreseeable circumstances. If they fail when applied, we have nowhere to go. So, for each emergency procedure there should be a plan for how it will be tested and how frequently. The test may be conducted as a desk-top exercise, as a pre-advised drill or as a surprise drill. First-aid response can be tested using scenarios and rescue procedures can make use of dummies with real equipment and possibly with pre-arranged involvement with the emergency services.

Fire Detection

The regulations require an appropriate form of fire detection and warning on construction sites. Note that workers can be an effective means of fire detection in many instances and are far more effective than automated detection systems in large open spaces or outside. However, there are times when automated fire detection is warranted. Picture a standard mess cabin with a kitchen at one end, tables and chairs in the middle section with a central door and a partitioned end section containing a drying room. Many cabins like this have mesh fitted over windows to prevent vandalism. Imagine a worker getting changed in the drying room at the same time as a fire starting in the kitchen area due to a faulty toaster. Without a smoke detector in the eating area, how would the worker know that a fire had started? If the fire spread to the central door, how would he get out?

Another situation that warrants fire detection is linked offices, particularly where those offices have internal partitions leaving rooms without access to final-exit doors. One further complication occurs when offices are double stacked. Take a common situation with just two cabins on site, one stacked on top of the other. They both have one central door and a steel staircase leading to the upper cabin. In most situations the lower cabin is the mess cabin and the upper one is the office/meeting room. Is it foreseeable that a fire in the mess cabin could develop to the point where flames lap up from the doorway to prevent escape from the upper cabin? Should a linked fire detection and warning system be fitted to both cabins?

A common error I have encountered on construction sites is the failure to test fire detection and warning systems. For some reason, some personnel on construction sites believe that 9V batteries in battery-powered smoke detectors are fair game for theft. Regular testing of the detectors picks this up and can nip it in the bud.

Also don't forget the situation where the existing fire detection and warning system in a building is either disabled temporarily or modified along with the structure. These situations need to be managed proactively to ensure continued coverage.

Fire Fighting
Given the range of ignition sources involved in construction work and the transient nature of fuel on site, it is unsurprising that fires occur. So, being able to extinguish small fires and create safe escape routes is essential. We all know about the need for fire extinguishers and that different types are suitable for dealing with different fuel types. What is less well known is that CDM requires every person (within reason) who works on a construction site and might need to use fire fighting measures to be give instruction in their safe use. Note that the requirement does not state 'training' but 'instruction'. In simple terms, this can be addressed as part of the induction process where workers receive a short instructional session on the safe use of extinguishers available to them without a practical demonstration. I use the mnemonic PASS to assist this process (Pull the pin, Aim the nozzle, Squeeze the handle, Sweep the nozzle) and a few do's and don'ts to achieve this instruction.

Chapter 12 – Transitional Arrangements and Brexit

The Health and Safety Executive recognised the need for transitional arrangements to cope with the period immediately after 6th April 2015. These arrangements explained how CDM 2015 applied to existing projects of varying sizes and at different stages as of 6th April 2015. However, the transitional arrangements were only in effect until 6th October 2015. This means that all construction projects must now comply with the full requirements of CDM 2015.

We have been informed by the HSE that leaving the European Union will have no immediate effect on health and safety legislation other than administrative changes to remove references to EU Directives.

###

You have reached the end of this book. Thank you for taking the time to read it and for the fact that you care enough to take your health and safety responsibilities seriously. I hope you found this book useful and look forward to hearing any feedback you may have.

Please send any correspondence to gavin.taylor@knutsfordsafety.co.uk.

For more information about the author and his work visit http://www.knutsfordsafety.co.uk.

About the Author

Gavin Taylor is a Chartered Safety and Health Practitioner, a Chartered Engineer, a member of the Association for Project Safety and a qualified teacher. He runs a health and safety consulting firm in Knutsford, Cheshire and works all over Great Britain and overseas helping organisations of all sizes to understand and comply with their duties under health and safety law. Gavin has written articles for the British Safety Council magazine, Safety Management, as well as delivering papers and presentations to health and safety conferences.

Gavin is a construction health and safety specialist (formerly a CDM coordinator) and has worked with companies including United Utilities, Bechtel, Cross Rail, Tube Lines, MWH, Costain, Carillion, Procter & Gamble, Northumbrian Water, Breedon Group, St. Modwen, Jaguar Land Rover and General Motors to improve their CDM and construction health and safety performance. He specialises in enabling companies to use a flexible and yet compliant approach to CDM without incurring unnecessary cost. Gavin also works with small companies to help them achieve cost-effective compliance with health and safety legislation beyond CDM.

If you want to know more about the Author or want help with any of the issues raised in this book, contact Gavin at Knutsford Safety LLP.

Printed in Great Britain
by Amazon

29997935R00040